CLINICAL EVALUATIONS FOR JUVENILES' COMPETENCE TO STAND TRIAL

A GUIDE FOR LEGAL PROFESSIONALS

Thomas Grisso

This guide for legal professionals is a companion for a guide that assists mental health professionals in their evaluations of youths' competence to stand trial:

Evaluating Juveniles' Adjudicative Competence: A Guide for Clinical Practice

Professional Resource Press
Sarasota, Florida

Published by
Professional Resource Press
(An Imprint of the Professional Resource Exchange, Inc.)
Post Office Box 3197
Sarasota, FL 34230-3197

Printed in the United States of America

The copy editor for this book was Patricia Rockwood, the managing editor was Debbie Fink, and the cover and text were designed by Laurie Girsch.

Library of Congress Cataloging-in-Publication Data

Grisso, Thomas.
    Clinical evaluations for juveniles' competence to stand trial : a guide for legal professionals / Thomas Grisso.
      p. cm.
    Includes bibliographical references.
    ISBN 10: 1-56887-097-3   ISBN 13: 978-1-56887-097-7
    1. Competency to stand trial--United States. 2. Criminal liability--United States. 3. Juvenile justice, Administration of--United States. I. Title.

KF9810.G75 2005
345.73'08--dc22

2005045905

ACKNOWLEDGMENTS

The development of this guide was supported by the John D. and Catherine T. MacArthur Foundation and accomplished as a project of the MacArthur Research Network on Adolescent Development and Juvenile Justice. That project included the development of a parallel guide for mental health examiners who evaluate juveniles' competence to stand trial, entitled *Evaluating Juveniles' Adjudicative Competence: A Guide for Clinical Practice* (also available from Professional Resource Press).

During the drafting of this guide for legal professionals, the author was advised by two members of the MacArthur Research Network that stimulated the work: developmental psychologist Laurence Steinberg (Chair of the Network) and Robert Schwartz, Director of the Juvenile Law Center. Additional research and reviewing were provided by Gina Vincent. Substantial consultation and advice were provided by district attorneys John Delaney (Pennsylvania) and Gus Sandstrom (Colorado), and defense attorney Curry Cook (Alaska).

The concepts in this guide for legal professionals were developed in the course of earlier preparation of the parallel clinicians' guide. Development of that work, which forms the foundation for the present one, involved the efforts of a wide range of professionals. They included:

- An initial working group – Richard Barnum, Barbara Kaban, Ann Tobey, and Jean Tomich – with extensive expertise in evaluations of juveniles in delinquency cases, especially for competence to stand trial
- Consulting juvenile court clinicians – Michael Barahal (Wisconsin), Michael Brannon (Florida), Patricia Carter (Missouri), Antoinette Kavanaugh (Illinois), Ivan Kruh (Washington), and Stephen McGraw (Florida)

- Consulting lawyers and judges – district attorneys John Delaney (Pennsylvania) and Gus Sandstrom (Colorado), The Honorable Ronald Alvarez (Florida), The Honorable Michael Corriero (New York), and defense attorneys Curry Cook (Alaska) and Laura Cohen (New Jersey)

Finally, members of the MacArthur Research Network on Adolescent Development and Juvenile Justice made general recommendations throughout the project. In addition to Dr. Steinberg and Mr. Schwartz, they included Marie Banich, Elizabeth Cauffman, Jeffrey Fagan, Sandra Graham, Amy Hehn, Patricia Lee, Orlando Martinez, Edward Mulvey, Daniel Nagin, Alex Piquero, Elizabeth Scott, Jennifer Woolard, Franklin Zimring, and Associate Member Alexes Harris.

The opinions and recommendations provided in this guide do not necessarily reflect those of the MacArthur Foundation or any of the individual professionals involved in the development and review of the guide.

TABLE OF CONTENTS

Part III

Understanding Clinicians' Evaluations

Part IV

Using Clinicians' Opinions

Part IV *(Continued)*

CLINICAL EVALUATIONS FOR JUVENILES' COMPETENCE TO STAND TRIAL

A GUIDE FOR LEGAL PROFESSIONALS

INTRODUCTION

The question of children's and adolescents' competence to stand trial was rarely raised in legal practice until the last decade of the 20th century.[1] For most of the history of the juvenile court, a juvenile's capacity to participate as a defendant in juvenile delinquency cases was not recognized as a legal necessity. Juvenile courts had a rehabilitative objective, justifying less need for a participating, decision-making defendant as a matter of due process. The issue was rarely raised in adult criminal courts, because most youths waived or transferred to criminal court were older adolescents very near the upper age of juvenile court jurisdiction.

Legal reforms in the 1990s, however, greatly increased the punitive consequences for youthful defendants when they were found delinquent. In addition, many states lowered the age for waiver or transfer to criminal court, so that younger adolescents could be tried "as adults." As a consequence, most jurisdictions in the U.S. began to experience a growing number of cases in which attorneys asked courts to determine whether their young clients had the requisite capacities associated with competence to stand trial – the ability to understand the proceedings and to assist counsel in a defense (as defined by the U.S. Supreme Court in *Dusky v. United States*[2]).

In contrast to juvenile court, the concept of competence to stand trial has a long history in criminal courts. Its purpose has been to protect defendants with mental illnesses or mental retardation from being tried unfairly. Their disabilities might jeopardize their defense if they impaired defendants' capacity to understand the trial process, the ability to make

---

[1] Richard Bonnie and Thomas Grisso, "Adjudicative Competence and Youthful Offenders," in *Youth on Trial: A Developmental Perspective on Juvenile Justice* (Thomas Grisso & Robert Schwartz [Eds.], 2000).
[2] 362 U.S. 402 (1960).

important decisions related to their defense, and the capacity to participate meaningfully in their adjudication.

THE PROBLEM

When applied to adolescents, the concept of competence to stand trial raises questions about youths' incapacities due not only to mental disorder or mental disability, but also to immaturity. Children and adolescents are in the process of acquiring adultlike levels of understanding and reasoning abilities. Therefore, at least some of them will not yet have the capacity to participate in their trials at a level that courts have required for competence to stand trial.

The notion of incompetence due to developmental immaturity is unavoidable when one applies the competence doctrine to defendants – some of them still in their elementary school years – who have not yet attained adult capacities. But this raises many questions. For example, at what age do most youths reach a level of understanding similar to adults? How can we tell when they have not? And is age even a relevant marker for judging legal competence? But before proceeding to address those questions, we should acknowledge the nature and limits of any answers we might find:

- Even if most youths are less mature than adults, this does not mean that most youths are incompetent to stand trial. Youths are not simply "mature" or "immature." They mature in degrees, so that many youths will have abilities that are sufficiently like those of adults to allow them to be considered competent to stand trial. Moreover, some may function as well as adults with respect to certain abilities (e.g., understanding the charges) but not others (e.g., being able to assist counsel).
- Asking about youths' potential incompetence to stand trial due to developmental immaturity is not the same as asking whether youths should be held criminally responsible for their illegal acts. In American jurisprudence, one's competence to stand trial (whether one's incapacities jeopardize the fairness of a trial) has always been a separate issue from criminal responsibility or culpability (whether one should be held responsible for a crime despite mental disorder or disability).

THE PURPOSE OF THIS GUIDE

Many of the questions of law and practice regarding youths' competence to stand trial are currently unresolved. As described later, they pertain to the legal definition, evaluation, and disposition of incompetence to stand trial in juvenile court. Moreover, criminal courts encounter many ambiguities regarding the role of developmental immaturity when judging youths' competence to stand trial in criminal court,[3] as well as about the appropriate response of the court to a finding of incompetence due to immaturity.

The information in this guide has been designed to assist judges and attorneys in the difficult task of working toward resolution of these issues. This guide does not describe how the issues of developmental immaturity and competence to stand trial should be resolved. Instead, it provides a structure to assist judges and attorneys when thinking about their competence to stand trial cases involving juveniles, recognizing that law evolves in part through case-by-case application.

This guide for legal professionals is the culmination of a project of the John D. and Catherine T. MacArthur Foundation. In 1996, the foundation convened a group of researchers – including science and legal professionals – who were charged with the task of studying the issue of juveniles' competence to stand trial. Their objective was to produce information that would assist the courts, attorneys, and child mental health examiners to consider the issue from a developmental perspective.

This group – the MacArthur Research Network on Adolescent Development and Juvenile Justice – worked together for 8 years to accomplish their project in three phases. In the first phase, the group produced a book that thoroughly reviewed the legal and psychological questions associated with the problem.[4] Second, they performed a nationwide scientific research study to learn about youths' actual abilities related to competence to stand trial, comparing youths of various ages to adults.[5] (The results of that study are discussed later.) Finally, the group

---

[3] Youths may be transferred or waived to stand trial in criminal court by a variety of means, depending on a state's laws: judicial discretionary transfer, statutory exclusion of juvenile adjudication based on certain ages and offenses, prosecutors' direct file, and other mechanisms. See generally, Robert Dawson, "Judicial Waiver in Theory and Practice," and Barry Feld, "Legislative Exclusion of Offenses From Juvenile Court Jurisdiction: A History and Critique" both in *The Changing Borders of Juvenile Justice: Transfer of Adolescents to the Criminal Court* (Jeffrey Fagan & Franklin Zimring [Eds.], 2000).

[4] Thomas Grisso and Robert Schwartz (Eds.), *Youth on Trial: A Developmental Perspective on Juvenile Justice* (2000).

[5] Thomas Grisso, Laurence Steinberg, et al., *Juveniles' Competence to Stand Trial: A Comparison of Adolescents' and Adults' Capacities as Trial Defendants*, 27 Law and Human Behavior 333 (2003).

created a number of documents, tools, and practice guides that would assist courts and child mental health clinicians in their application of the competence concept to adolescents. Those documents were developed with the assistance of a number of national panels of legal and child forensic mental health consultants. One of their products was a practice manual for mental health professionals, *Evaluating Juveniles' Adjudicative Competence: A Guide for Clinical Practice.*[6] It offers concepts and specific methods for performing evaluations of youths when their competence to stand trial is questioned in juvenile or criminal court.

The present guide for judges and lawyers is designed to accompany the practice guide for mental health professionals. It describes the same legal and developmental concepts. It also provides an overview of the methods and logic that are being recommended to mental health professionals who perform evaluations of juveniles when questions of their legal competence are raised. It aims to improve legal professionals' understanding of the information that mental health professionals offer in cases involving minors' competence to stand trial, whether in juvenile or in criminal court.

The guide has four main sections. Part I describes the concept of competence to stand trial and the primary issues that arise when the concept is invoked with respect to juveniles. Part II describes developmental and clinical concepts that can guide mental health professionals' evaluations of juveniles for competence to stand trial. Part III describes the process of a juvenile competence case, including when to raise the question and what to expect of clinicians when they are asked to perform competence evaluations of juveniles. Finally, Part IV offers guidance for legal professionals in understanding the nature of mental health examiners' opinions about the results of their evaluations of juveniles' abilities related to competence.

Footnotes in the guide do not include citations to all relevant legal cases and statutes in all U.S. jurisdictions. Instead, the guide references other works that have compiled comprehensive citations to relevant state and federal laws, as well as legal reviews and social science research reviews. Law is developing rapidly in this area; comprehensive reviews of laws at the time of publication of this guide may have a short shelf-life. Readers are encouraged to consult up-to-date legal reviews in the years following the publication of this guide.

---

[6] Thomas Grisso, *Evaluating Juveniles' Adjudicative Competence: A Guide for Clinical Practice* (2005).

Part I

THE LEGAL STANDARD AND PROCESS

This part describes the legal definition of competence to stand trial, application of the law in criminal and juvenile court, and legal disposition for cases in which defendants are found incompetent. It describes the current status of the law, while identifying a number of legal questions that have not yet been resolved in many jurisdictions. Legal professionals must consult their own jurisdiction's laws and practices for the specific application of these matters in their own courts.

WHAT IS THE LEGAL STANDARD?

All states define the legal standard for competence to stand trial in a manner consistent with the U.S. Supreme Court's definition in *Dusky v. U.S.*[7] and affirmed in *Godinez v. Moran*:[8] whether the defendant has "sufficient present ability to consult with his lawyer with a reasonable degree of rational understanding" and whether the defendant has a "rational as well as factual understanding of proceedings against him." Several points are important regarding the application of this standard in juvenile court.

First, *competence to stand trial is recognized as a requisite for due process in delinquency cases in a majority of states.*[9] And, of course, competence is required of youths being tried in criminal court just as for adults. Second, *the Dusky standard is the definition of competence to*

---

[7] 362 U.S. 402 (1960).

[8] 113 S.Ct. 2680 (1993).

[9] Richard Redding and Linda Frost, *Adjudicative Competence in the Modern Juvenile Court,* 9 Virginia Journal of Social Policy and Law 353 (2001); Richard Bonnie and Thomas Grisso, supra note 1.

stand trial in delinquency cases. All states that have addressed the question have concluded that the *Dusky* standard, originally fashioned for criminal courts, applies also for inquiries about competence in juvenile court.[10]

Third, some statutes and analyses of appellate cases have provided guidance regarding the specific types of abilities associated with the two broad categories in the *Dusky* standard.[11] If the *Dusky* standard applies in juvenile court, it is reasonable to assume that *the specific types of abilities used by criminal courts to assess competence apply in juvenile court as well.* These specific abilities are discussed later, when clinicians' evaluations are described. In general practice,[12] they include the defendant's understanding and appreciation of the charges, potential pleas, and their consequences; an understanding and appreciation of the roles of various participants in the trial process; the ability to understand communications from counsel and to be able to communicate meaningfully with counsel in developing a defense; the ability to understand, appreciate, and make decisions about the waiver of important rights, especially decisions about pleading and plea agreements; and the ability to testify at trial if necessary. The relevant abilities do not pertain only to the formal trial – they refer to the defendant's role in all stages of the process, including arraignment, pleading, attorney consultation, and the trial on the evidence.

Fourth, although the *Dusky* standard applies in both criminal and juvenile courts, *it is unclear in most jurisdictions whether the same threshold of ability is required in juvenile court as in criminal court.*[13] Although it is clear that the same general abilities are weighed, it is unclear whether a competent defendant in juvenile court must have the same degree or extent of those abilities as a competent defendant in criminal court. Must youths in delinquency cases be as capable as the average adult in a criminal case, or is it sufficient for them to be as capable as the average youth in juvenile court? These matters have only begun to be addressed by courts.[14] They will be resolved as a matter of law in the course of future adjudication of juvenile competency cases.

---

[10] Richard Redding and Linda Frost, id. Elizabeth Scott and Thomas Grisso, *Developmental Incompetence, Due Process, and Juvenile Justice Policy,* 83 North Carolina Law Review 101 (2005).

[11] For an example in the Florida statutes, see: FL. R. Crim. Pro. § 3.211(a). See generally, Thomas Grisso, *Evaluating Competencies: Forensic Assessments and Instruments* (2nd ed., 2003).

[12] See Thomas Grisso, id.

[13] Elizabeth Scott and Thomas Grisso, supra note 10.

[14] For example, see: *State v. Settles,* 1998 Ohio App. LEXIS 4973, 9 (1998); *People v. Carey,* 615 N.W.2d 742 (Mich.App. 2000).

Finally, in most states, *the law is silent regarding developmental immaturity as a legally accepted cause for incompetence to stand trial.* Typically courts must have evidence regarding the cause of a defendant's deficits in the abilities noted previously.[15] Historically, serious mental illness and/or mental retardation have been the most common reasons for deficits in abilities resulting in findings of incompetence. In these cases, the test of competence is a functional test of the defendant's genuine abilities and not simply a diagnosis of mental illness or retardation. As described later, however, in some adolescent cases, deficits in such abilities may also arise because a youth's cognitive or decision-making capacities have not yet matured sufficiently to meet the threshold for competence. A few states have recognized developmental immaturity as a potential cause for incompetence,[16] and a recent survey suggests that developmental immaturity is being recognized in practice in many juvenile courts.[17] But most states have not settled the issue as a matter of law. It is likely, however, that age alone cannot be used as a proxy for incompetence, only as an explanation for apparent deficits in abilities.

WHAT IS THE LEGAL PROCESS?

Raising the Question

In most states, the question of competence may be raised by the judge, district attorney, or defense attorney. Laws recognize these parties as having an obligation to raise the question of competence whenever there is any doubt that the defendant might have deficits in abilities related to competence to stand trial.[18]

Ordering the Evaluation

When the question is raised, typically the court orders an investigation by a mental health examiner (usually a psychologist or psychiatrist) who performs an evaluation focused specifically on obtaining data related to competence. Examiners must be familiar with the legal criteria for

---

[15] Some causes do not warrant a finding of incompetence – for example, when defendants simply lack familiarity with the nature of trials (in which case their attorneys might be able to instruct them without the need for a finding of incompetence).

[16] For example, Florida: FL. STAT. § 985.223(1)(h)(2).

[17] Thomas Grisso and Judith Quinlan, *Juvenile Court Clinical Services: A National Description,* University of Massachusetts Medical School, Worcester, MA. (Available at Thomas.Grisso@umassmed.edu)

[18] *Pate v. Robinson,* 383 U.S. 375 (1966).

competence to stand trial. When the defendant is a juvenile, courts may recognize the importance of the examiner's experience in the clinical and developmental assessment of children and adolescents (as should be required; see Part II).

Course of the Evaluation

Most states' competency laws require that the competence evaluation must be completed, and results reported to the court, within a specified period of time (e.g., 10, 20, or 30 days), with the potential for requesting an extension of the time period under extraordinary circumstances. Examiners prepare written reports of competence evaluations in virtually all competence evaluation cases. Part III describes the manner in which competence evaluations of juveniles should be performed. It also describes ways in which the defense attorney may wish to monitor the evaluation process.

Hearing on Competence

In many juvenile courts (and criminal courts), formal hearings on the evidence provided by the competence evaluation are unnecessary when the defense attorney and the district attorney agree on the results of the evaluation. Otherwise, a hearing is provided to allow evidence to be presented. If the court finds that the youth is competent to stand trial, the adjudicative process continues (e.g., a court date is set for adjudication of the charges). If the court finds that the youth is incompetent to stand trial, the court should inquire of the mental health examiner (a) whether deficits in the youth's competence-relevant abilities can be remediated within a reasonable period of time (usually specified by statute, and often being 1 year), and if so, (b) what will be necessary in order to accomplish remediation.

Disposition for Finding of Incompetence

If the youth's incompetence is potentially remediable within the time provided by law, the court orders an appropriate referral for remediation services. For youths whose incompetence is related to mental illness, this may take the form of inpatient or outpatient psychiatric treatment appropriate for children or adolescents. For youths whose incompetence is due to mental retardation or developmental immaturity, the proper remediation is far less certain in most jurisdictions. Some states[19] have

---

[19] For example, Florida: Annette McGaha et al., *Juveniles Adjudicated Incompetent to Proceed: A Descriptive Study of Florida's Competence Restoration Program*, 29 Journal of the American Academy of Psychiatry and Law, 427 (2001).

special programs designed to increase youths' capacities related to competence to stand trial through special educational efforts focused specifically on the abilities associated with the *Dusky* standard. Most communities do not have such programs, however, which increases the likelihood that youths found incompetent due to mental retardation or developmental immaturity might have to be deemed unremediable. As described in Part II, youths' incompetence due to developmental immaturity often involves capacities (e.g., decision-making abilities) that are unlikely to be improved by time-limited instruction, because they require substantial time for cognitive or psychosocial maturation before those abilities can be nurtured. (For further discussion, see Part IV.)

If the court finds that the youth's incompetence is not likely to be remediated within the statutory time period, the charges must be dismissed and the delinquency (or criminal) proceeding terminated, often with some further action.[20] For example, sometimes civil proceedings arise at this point (such as civil commitment to psychiatric inpatient treatment), and some statutes offer the specific option of assigning custody of the youth to programs in the juvenile court's child welfare system.[21] Most states' laws, however, do not yet provide clear directives to apply in formulating dispositions specifically for juveniles whose competence is judged nonremediable.

A further point that is unsettled in many courts is the disposition of youths found incompetent to stand trial in criminal court (after having been waived or transferred for trial as an adult). Some courts remand such youths to juvenile court for adjudication of their charges. However, as noted earlier, some juvenile courts interpret the threshold of capacity for competence to be the same in juvenile court as in criminal court. In those courts, youths found incompetent in criminal court and returned to juvenile court will also be incompetent in juvenile court. This dilemma less often arises, however, in courts that apply a less stringent threshold for competence in juvenile court.[22]

---

[20] For a review of state statutes regarding dispositions when juveniles are found incompetent, see Richard Redding and Linda Frost, supra note 9.

[21] For example, Arkansas and Virginia statutes: see Richard Redding and Linda Frost, supra note 9.

[22] For a discussion of this dilemma, see Elizabeth Scott and Thomas Grisso, supra note 10.

Part II

TAKING A DEVELOPMENTAL PERSPECTIVE

Youths' competence to stand trial requires attention to certain psychological and clinical factors that are different from those encountered in competence evaluations for adults. These factors derive from the fact that youths are still developing various cognitive and social capacities that they will someday have as adults. Part II reviews some of the clinical and psychological factors that mental health examiners consider when they are performing competence evaluations with juveniles.

WHAT MENTAL DISORDERS ARE RELEVANT?

Many mental disorders of childhood and adolescence are different from those of adulthood. When adult defendants are found incompetent to stand trial due to mental disorder, typically the disorders involved are psychotic conditions that include gross distortions of reality or severe depression. In contrast, youths' abilities associated with competence to stand trial can be impaired as a consequence of various mental disorders that do not involve psychotic thinking.

For example, a youth's ADHD (Attention-Deficit/Hyperactivity Disorder) may be so severe that the youth cannot focus attention on matters related to the trial process. Anxiety disorders may cause some youths to withdraw so extremely that they cannot exercise adequate involvement in their consultation with their attorney or their decision making about a plea agreement. Learning disabilities may greatly reduce youths' capacities to grasp the significance of trial events as they unfold. The point is not that these disorders always produce these effects on abilities relevant for the competence question. But a greater range and type of disorders may impair youths' abilities compared to adults.

Therefore, it is very important that mental health examiners conduct a careful and thorough clinical evaluation of youths in competence evaluations, in order to attend to the range of disorders that might interfere with youths' abilities associated with competence.

WHAT IS MEANT BY "IMMATURITY" AS A THREAT TO COMPETENCE?

There are two main types of maturation that are relevant when considering youths' competence to stand trial: cognitive and psychosocial.

Cognitive maturation refers to one's capacity to understand and process information. For example, adults typically are capable of thinking "abstractly." They can form a "concept" of the defense attorney as one who has a role that involves assistance to a defendant, and they can form a notion of a right that includes being entitled to decide whatever they want, no matter what authority figures would wish. Some youths, however, have not yet developed the ability to form an abstract concept. Until they are older, they think more "concretely" – that is, based on what they can actually see or experience at that moment. To them, a right may simply be something that authority figures allow them to do, but which authority can just as easily take away. Other aspects of cognitive maturity include the ability to handle complex information, especially tracking how one event influences another in a trial process, or dealing with plea agreements that have a variety of pros and cons.

Cognitive maturation is related in part to age – on average, 12 year olds will be less mature in these abilities than 16 year olds. *But it is not safe to presume that a youth is at a particular level of cognitive maturation on the basis of age alone.* Some 16 year olds with mental retardation, developmental delays, or ADHD are much like the average 12 year old in terms of cognitive maturation. And there are 12 year olds whose cognitive abilities are greatly advanced for their age. Generally speaking, however, the cognitive abilities of individuals younger than 15 or 16 are less developed relative to those who are 16 and older.

Psychosocial maturation refers to factors that have more to do with "perspective" in practical, social situations, especially when one is making decisions or reacting to problems. Some psychosocial factors that are still developing in adolescents include:

- *Risk Perception*: Many youths are poorer at perceiving and evaluating risk than they will be when they reach maturity.

- *Self-Directedness*: Many youths are more influenced by what they believe their peers would approve, rather than weighing the issues in a self-directed, independent way.
- *Time Perspective*: Many youths make decisions based mostly on short-term outcomes rather than considering the longer range consequences, more so than when they become adults.

Youths' immaturity with regard to these perspectives sometimes has a significant influence on their interpretations of the trial process, their relation with their attorney, and their decisions about pleas and plea agreements. For example, an individual who is limited in judging risks or considering the longer term consequences of his or her decisions may have difficulty evaluating the costs and benefits of a particular plea agreement. Other examples are provided in Part IV.

DOES IMMATURITY
MAKE A DIFFERENCE?

Whether developmental factors need to be taken into account when thinking about youths' capacities related to competence to stand trial depends partly on whether there is substantial evidence that those factors are related to the abilities in question in competency cases. Several recent studies have examined adolescents' and adults' abilities associated with competence to stand trial, in some cases comparing them to those of adults.[23] Despite the fact that the studies vary considerably in their ways of assessing youths' competency abilities, their results have been quite consistent. A brief description of one of these studies, conducted by the

---

[23] For example: D. Baerger, E. Griffin, J. Lyons, and R. Simmons, *Competency to Stand Trial in Preadjudicated and Petitioned Juvenile Defendants,* 31 Journal of the American Academy of Psychiatry and Law 314 (2003). D. Burnett, C. Noblin, and V. Prosser, *Adjudicative Competency in a Juvenile Population,* 31 Criminal Justice and Behavior 438 (2004). T. Grisso, L. Steinberg, J. Woolard, E. Cauffman, E. Scott, S. Graham, F. Lexcen, N. Reppucci, and R. Schwartz, *Juveniles' Competence to Stand Trial: A Comparison of Adolescents' and Adults' Capacities as Trial Defendants,* 27 Law and Human Behavior 333 (2003). G. McKee and S. Shea, *Competency to Stand Trial in Family Court: Characteristics of Competent and Incompetent Juveniles,* 27 Journal of the American Academy of Psychiatry and Law 65 (1999). A. Redlich, M. Silverman, and H. Steiner, *Pre-Adjudicative and Adjudicative Competence in Juveniles and Youth Adults,* 21 Behavioral Sciences and the Law 393 (2003). J. Schmidt, N. Reppucci, and J. Woolard, *Effectiveness of Participation as a Defendant: The Attorney-Juvenile Client Relationship,* 21 Behavioral Sciences and the Law 175 (2003). J. Warren, J. Aaron, E. Ryan, P. Chauhan, and J. DuVal, *Correlates of Adjudicative Competence Among Psychiatrically Impaired Juveniles,* 31 Journal of the American Academy of Psychiatry and Law 299 (2003).

MacArthur Research Network on Adolescent Development and Juvenile Justice,[24] will demonstrate those findings.

The study examined the abilities of 927 adolescents (ages 12 to 17) in juvenile detention facilities and community settings, comparing their abilities to 466 young adults (ages 18 to 24) in jails and in the community. Four communities in different parts of the U.S. were involved in the study. Among the various tests that youths and adults completed was an instrument[25] that assesses abilities to understand information relevant for trials and assisting counsel in a defense, as well as abilities to reason about the relevance of evidence for trials and about decisions that defendants often must make in the course of the trial process. The instrument uses highly objective scoring of individuals' responses, and it allows for comparison of youths' performance to that of groups of adults in past studies who had or had not been found incompetent to stand trial. Other instruments in the research study assessed youths' and adults' choices, and their reasoning about those choices, when told a story in which a defendant had to make a decision about waiver of rights at arrest, about working with an attorney, and about accepting or rejecting a plea agreement.

In the MacArthur study, youths aged 15 and younger performed more poorly on average than did young adults, with a greater proportion manifesting a level of impairment consistent with that of adults in past research who had been found incompetent to stand trial. One-third of youths aged 13 and younger manifested a significant level of impairment on the measure of competency abilities. For youths aged 13 and younger who also had intelligence test scores below 75, about one-half had significantly impaired performance. Youths 16 and 17 years old on average were no different from adults in their performance.

Adolescents also tended to make different choices in legally relevant decisions than did adults. For example, the younger the adolescents were, the more likely they were to accept a proffered plea agreement and to make other decisions that complied with authority. Moreover, their reasons for doing so tended to be more superficial and less focused on longer range outcomes, suggesting decision making that was related to immaturity in time perspective and risk assessment.

Perhaps the most important implication of the results of this study is that many youths – more often than adults – manifested deficits in abilities related to trial participation that are similar to those of adults who are

---

[24] Thomas Grisso, Laurence Steinberg, et al., supra note 23.

[25] Norman Poythress et al., *The MacArthur Competence Assessment Tool-Criminal Adjudication: Professional Manual* (MacCAT-CA: 1999).

found incompetent to stand trial due to mental disorders. These youths' deficits, however, were not related to mental disorder but to the fact that they were simply operating with cognitive and psychological abilities that had not yet matured.

WHAT IS DIFFERENT ABOUT EVALUATING YOUTHS' COMPETENCE TO STAND TRIAL?

Studies such as this one have provided insight into the ages at which youths are more greatly at risk of poor abilities that are relevant for the question of competence to stand trial. Just as important, however, they have provided suggestions for the ways in which mental health examiners' competency evaluations of juveniles should be implemented. Part III will describe some of the special features of these evaluations, but the following are some of the general and more important points:

- Juvenile competence to stand trial evaluations should be performed by mental health professionals who are specialized not only in evaluations for forensic questions, but also are specialized in the diagnosis of children's mental disorders and the assessment of youths' developmental capacities.
- Special sources of information are needed for evaluations of youths' competence, sources that are less often seen in adult competency evaluations. For example, examiners should obtain and review, whenever possible, past records from a youth's school, physician, or mental health service provider.[26] In addition, it is always necessary for mental health examiners to obtain information directly from caretakers (parents, relatives, foster parents) regarding the youth's past and current development.
- Past studies have found that when youths seem to understand some point about trials, too often this understanding is only "factual" or superficial. The *Dusky* standard speaks also of "rational" understanding. This is often called "appreciation" by many mental health competency examiners, referring to the individual's ability to appreciate the significance of what he or she knows. For example, imagine that a youth tells us that "the defense attorney is someone who helps you during your trial."

---

[26] It is better to obtain such information directly from the source to avoid any possible editing, or allegation of editing, by an intermediary such as a parent, attorney, or probation officer.

Knowing this, however, is of little significance if the youth does not understand how the attorney can help, or that the attorney will help even if the charges are true, or that the prosecutor, while also an attorney, has a very different role in the proceeding. Many youths believe that defense counsel "helps the innocent" but must inform the court if the client actually "did the crime."[27] Mental health competency examiners often refer to the latter as a lack of "appreciation" or "rational understanding," despite adequate factual understanding.

- Juvenile and adult competency evaluations must focus in part on the *clinical* status of the defendant (e.g., the presence of mental disorder), but juvenile competency evaluations must also determine the *developmental* status of the defendant. This requires special attention to the youth's cognitive and psychosocial status in relation to peers and/or adults.[28]

In summary, a developmental perspective is very important when evaluating youths' competence to stand trial. Their younger developmental status has implications for the types of mental disorders that may impair their abilities, and their "normal" developmental status – in terms of cognitive and psychosocial development – may explain deficits in their understanding and reasoning about important matters in the trial process. Finally, as Part III discusses in more detail, youths' lesser maturity requires somewhat different assessment methods than are typical for competence to stand trial evaluations for adults.

---

[27] Thomas Grisso, *Juveniles' Waiver of Rights: Legal and Psychological Competence* (1981).

[28] As noted in Part I, a comparison to adults is appropriate when youths are being evaluated for potential adjudication in criminal court, but whether they should be compared to adults or to their peers is less clear as a matter of law in juvenile court.

Part III

UNDERSTANDING CLINICIANS' EVALUATIONS

This part is intended to inform legal professionals regarding what they should expect from mental health examiners' evaluations in competence to stand trial cases involving juveniles, and to suggest ways in which legal professionals can contribute to competency evaluations that will be of greatest benefit to all parties and the court. There is no standard way to perform competence evaluations with juveniles, so the following does not describe clinicians' actual practice. Instead, it describes the practices that are recommended for clinicians in the guide for clinicians – mentioned in the Introduction – that accompanies the present guide for legal professionals.

THE REFERRAL

Raising the Question

The process begins when the court, defense counsel, or prosecutor raises the question of the youth's competence to stand trial. Law in one's jurisdiction may indicate when the question should be raised.[29] From a clinical perspective, current research regarding the abilities of adolescents suggests that *any one* of the following factors should alert courts and attorneys to the possible need to raise the question of a youth's competence to stand trial:

---

[29] For example, Virginia requires that the competency question must be raised for any juvenile who is being considered for transfer to criminal court: Va. Code Ann. §16.1-269.1(A).

- The youth has a prior diagnosis of mental illness serious enough to have required treatment in the past, or the youth has a prior diagnosis of mental retardation.
- The youth has a prior record of having performed very poorly on intelligence tests (e.g., IQ score below 75) or has a school record indicating a learning disability.
- The youth is 13 years of age or younger.
- During any contacts (pretrial, or at trial), the youth's behavior has been suggestive of deficits in memory, attention, or interpretation of reality.

Identifying the Examiner

Most juvenile courts have mental health professionals who are designated to perform competence to stand trial evaluations when provided a court order, although these arrangements differ considerably across jurisdictions.[30] Some juvenile courts have clinics within the court itself, others obtain their evaluations from local mental health centers, and many use private practitioners in the community. When attorneys seek competence evaluations independently, they should make sure that the examiner with whom they contract has adequate qualifications for evaluating children (which cannot be presumed merely because the examiner is a psychiatrist or psychologist) and is very familiar with the special requirements of competence to stand trial evaluations.

Specifying the Referral Question

When courts or attorneys assign examiners the task of performing a competence to stand trial evaluation, the referral should clearly state (a) that this is the purpose of the evaluation and (b) the relevant legal requirements, if any, regarding how and when the evaluation should be performed (e.g., allowable time limits). In addition, if at all possible, it is helpful for the referral to include a brief statement (one or two sentences) indicating the reason that the question was raised (e.g., one or more of the factors described above as potential reasons to raise the question). This helps the examiner to choose evaluation methods that will answer those concerns specifically (e.g., paying special attention to diagnosis of certain types of disorders when the court observed that "the youth was acting and talking strangely"). Finally, in their referrals for evaluations, many courts are able to order access to relevant records that the examiner might need to perform the evaluation.

---

[30] Thomas Grisso and Judith Quinlan, supra note 17.

EXAMINER'S PREPARATION
FOR THE EVALUATION

Examiners engage in several activities before proceeding to interview youths in competence evaluations. The following are some of those activities that are of special importance for defense counsel.

Course of Evaluations

Examiners initially establish some plan for the evaluation based on their need to obtain adequate information within the limits provided by law and circumstances. "Adequate" information may vary from case to case, but as described below, often it will require a plan (and time) for obtaining records from other agencies, making appointments with youth and caretakers for interviews and possible psychological testing, and preparation of a written report. Examiners are encouraged to meet with youths more than once during an evaluation. Youths' behaviors and emotions at a first interview often are influenced by the newness of the situation and unfamiliarity with the examiner, so that second interviews often reveal features of the youth that were not apparent in the first contact. As noted later, second interviews also are often helpful in determining youths' capacities to learn and retain relevant information that was provided them in the first interview.

Balancing these needs against practical constraints can be very difficult for mental health examiners. Law or policy in some jurisdictions typically place a time limit on the evaluation. It is in neither the court's nor the youth's interest to unduly delay the trial process during the performance of a competence evaluation. However, when this time requirement is very brief (e.g., 5 working days), inevitably the range of information that the examiner can collect will be compromised. In addition, some courts have financial arrangements for evaluations that compensate examiners for only 1 or 2 hours of their time. This is far shorter than the average amount of time that most experienced examiners believe is necessary in order to perform juvenile competence evaluations thoroughly and carefully.[31] Some courts may wish to review their policies to determine whether they are providing conditions that promote quality in examiners' information for the courts in juvenile competence cases.

---

[31] A recent survey of 87 juvenile court clinical services nationwide found that their examiners spent, on average, about 8 hours in data collection and report writing for their juvenile competence to stand trial evaluations. Thomas Grisso and Judith Quinlan, supra note 17.

Notifying Defense Counsel

The accompanying practice guide for mental health examiners recommends that they contact the youth's defense counsel soon after receiving a court order for a competence to stand trial evaluation. Often the youth's attorney will already know that the evaluation has been ordered, but in some jurisdictions the referral occurs even before defense counsel has become involved in the case. Notifying the attorney provides the opportunity for protection of the youth's rights during the evaluation process. In most jurisdictions, however, examiners are not obligated to provide such notification or to obtain counsel's approval before proceeding with the evaluation; the practice guide simply recommends it as a matter of professional practice. Whether the attorney replies when an examiner has left a telephone message is a matter left to the attorney's discretion. But it is recommended that attorneys do so, especially in order to address other matters affecting the youth's welfare, as described in the following discussions.

Seeking Information
From Defense Counsel

Examiners often can perform better evaluations if they can obtain some information from defense counsel regarding the youth prior to meeting with the youth. For example, if the youth's attorney has raised the question of competence, contact with the attorney allows the examiner to learn more about the attorney's observations of the youth that suggested the need for an evaluation. The practice guide for examiners includes an "Attorney CST Questionnaire" that some examiners may wish to send to the attorney requesting such information. Whether defense counsel responds to this questionnaire is, of course, a matter of discretion, taking into consideration the pros and cons of providing such information in light of the youth's legal interests.

Examiners often begin their evaluation process by determining what records might be available regarding the youth's academic and mental health history. Such records often contain information bearing on intellectual or emotional problems that are relevant for the competence question. Often it is very difficult for examiners to obtain these records in a timely fashion. Sometimes defense counsel is in a position to facilitate this process (e.g., requesting the court's assistance in obtaining records, or working with youths' caretakers to obtain them), and sometimes counsel already has such records. Attorneys should consider the potential value, in the youth's interest, of facilitating examiners' access to historical records that may be important to document the youth's disabilities. Whenever possible, the best practice is to obtain the records directly from the source, to avoid challenges regarding alterations of records obtained via other parties.

Defense Counsel's Option to Attend the Evaluation Interviews

Some jurisdictions allow youths' defense counsel to attend the competence evaluation. Defense attorneys sometimes wish to do so, in order to observe for themselves the examiner's process and to assure maximum protection of the youth's rights. Some examiners may be resistant to the defense attorney's presence at the evaluation, but the accompanying guide for examiners discusses the potential benefits of this arrangement. For example, some examiners see value in asking the attorney and the youth to engage in a quasi-consultative conversation at some point in the evaluation, so that the examiner can actually observe the youth's capacity to receive and communicate information while interacting with counsel (one of the abilities associated with competence to stand trial). Some attorneys welcome this, while others will object to discussing case-related information with the youth in the presence of the examiner (based on concerns about confidentiality in the attorney-client relationship).

As these comments suggest, there are differences of opinion among examiners and attorneys alike regarding the role of counsel during a juvenile's competence evaluation. The practice guide for examiners does not recommend how these differences should be resolved. It simply suggests that there are good reasons for the diverse perspectives. Examiners and attorneys should thoughtfully consider the options and their various benefits and risks while forming opinions about the best course.

Notifying the Caretaker And the Youth

The examiners' practice guide strongly encourages mental health examiners to involve caretakers (parents, guardians) in the youth's competence evaluation whenever possible. As explained later, interviews with caretakers often provide some of the most important information about a youth's developmental history and current abilities. Sometimes the inclusion of caretakers is simply not feasible, however, and their absence does not automatically mean that the evaluation is inferior in quality. But the value of having their input during the evaluation is sufficiently important that attorneys should question examiners when they do not include caretakers in the evaluation process.

EVALUATING YOUTHS' CLINICAL AND DEVELOPMENTAL HISTORY AND STATUS

The term "clinical" refers to significant issues of health, physical injuries and diseases, mental disorders, mental retardation, substance use disorders, and any past or current treatment for such conditions. The term "developmental" is not completely distinct from "clinical," but signifies a focus on the maturation process across the youth's past, as well as the degree of maturation that the youth currently has achieved in relation to peers. Some aspects of development go beyond "clinical" conditions – for example, the degree to which the youth is advanced, average, or delayed (compared to same-age peers) in social skills, problem-solving abilities, and the various psychosocial factors discussed in Part II. For both clinical and developmental characteristics of the youth, "history" refers to the youth's *past* behavior or mental conditions. "Status" refers to the youth's *current* behavior, mental conditions, and abilities.

The practice guide for juvenile competence examiners provides interview guides that they can use to structure their collection of clinical and developmental information for youths. There is no one way to obtain such information, however, and examiners may employ other methods from their general clinical experience with children and families.

Historical Information

Mental health examiners will want to obtain historical information regarding the youth's past health and mental health conditions, including past treatments for mental disorders, in almost all competence evaluations. Typically this will require that they interview the caretaker and youth about those conditions, obtain relevant records from various sources (e.g., hospitals and schools), and sometimes make direct contact with mental health professionals who have had contact with the youth in the past. Information regarding the youth's past development of cognitive and social abilities sometimes involves using more wide-ranging sources. In addition to obtaining a history from caretakers, examiners might talk to teachers, relatives, or social service workers to build a chronological picture of the youth's development.

Current Status Information

The youth's current clinical and developmental status typically is based on the examiner's direct, face-to-face observations of the youth. Special methods are often used during interviews with youths to assess their current status. For example, most examiners employ a "mental status exam." This is a standard set of clinical questions designed to check on a wide range of possible behaviors, thoughts, and emotions that might reveal symptoms of mental or emotional disorder. The practice guide for examiners' competence to stand trial evaluations also contains an interview guide for obtaining data about youths' current status regarding psychosocial development.

Psychological Testing

Some examiners use psychological tests to supplement their direct observations of youths' current mental or developmental status. Examples include intelligence tests (e.g., Wechsler Intelligence Scale for Children-4th ed.), measures of academic achievement (e.g., Wide Range Achievement Test-3), or measures of personality or mental disorder (e.g., Minnesota Multiphasic Personality Inventory-Adolescent).[32] Examiners who use psychological tests do not (and need not) do so for every case. The preferred approach is to determine whether the case itself raises specific questions that require an objective assessment of some feature of mental disorder, personality characteristic, or intellectual functioning. Typically this will happen when interviews and records do not provide an obvious answer to a clinical or developmental question that the examiner believes is very important for understanding the youth's competence abilities.

Feigning Symptoms or
Deficits in Abilities ("Malingering")

Clinicians should be alert to the possibility that youths might feign ("malinger") symptoms of mental disorder. Instruments have been developed to identify possible feigning of symptoms of mental disorder in adults, but their value with adolescents is largely unknown. Some of the comprehensive instruments that assess adolescent disorders have scales

---

[32] For a review of many clinical and forensic assessment instruments often used by clinicians in evaluations in delinquency cases, see: Thomas Grisso, Gina Vincent, and Daniel Seagrave (Eds.), *Mental Health Screening and Assessment in Juvenile Justice* (2005).

that seek to identify exaggeration in the reporting of symptoms, such as might arise in cases in which youths are feigning disorders.[33]

EVALUATING YOUTHS' COMPETENCY ABILITIES

Every evaluation for youths' competence to stand trial must provide information regarding youths' actual understanding and appreciation of matters that are represented in the Dusky *standard.* The accompanying guide for examiners' evaluation in juvenile competence offers a structured interview for examiners to use in order to collect this information. The interview, called the "Juvenile Adjudicative Competence Interview" (JACI), was designed especially to cover the range of abilities associated with the *Dusky* standard. Moreover, it does this in a manner that is sensitive to the types of deficits in relevant abilities that may be due to youths' developmental status. The following discussions use the JACI to illustrate important features of an appropriate examination of youths' abilities related to competence to stand trial.

Types of Abilities
Requiring Assessment

The JACI is a set of interview questions covering the topic areas shown in the accompanying table (p. 25). For each area, the JACI provides several questions that the examiner asks the youth, offering the examiner evidence for the youth's grasp of the matters in question. For most of the topic areas, the JACI includes two types of questions.

Understanding questions help the examiner assess the youth's basic knowledge of facts and procedures in the adjudication process (related to "factual understanding" in the legal standard). For example, "What is the defense lawyer's job?" or "What does a probation officer do?"

In contrast, *Appreciation* questions are designed to assist the examiner in assessing youths' perceptions and beliefs about the implications of the factual information (related to "rational understanding" in the legal standard). For example, given that the youth understands that the defense attorney "helps" the defendant, "What are some of the *ways* in which the attorney might help the defendant?" or "In a trial, how would your

---

[33] For a useful text on malingering in adolescent cases, see: Joseph McCann, *Malingering and Deception in Adolescents: Assessing Credibility in Clinical and Forensic Settings* (1998).

TOPIC AREAS FOR QUESTIONING IN THE JUVENILE ADJUDICATIVE COMPETENCE INTERVIEW (JACI)

Nature and Purpose of the Trial

- Nature and seriousness of offense
- Nature and purpose of the juvenile court trial
- Possible pleas
- Guilt and punishment/penalties

Roles of Participants

- Role of the prosecutor
- Role of the juvenile defense lawyer
- Role of the probation officer
- Role of the juvenile court judge
- (Optional: Role of the jury)

Assisting Counsel

- Assisting the defense attorney
- Plea bargains/agreements

Reasoning and Decision Making

- Deciding about having a defense lawyer
- Deciding how to assist your lawyer
- Deciding how to plead
- Deciding about a plea bargain

Participating at the Juvenile Court Hearing

- Ability to attend to events
- Ability to maintain self-control
- Ability to testify

probation officer be different from your lawyer?" The importance of pursuing both "factual understanding" and "rational understanding" (appreciation) is explained further in Part IV.

Exploring "Capacity" to Understand and Appreciate

When youths fail to understand some element in the JACI interview, the JACI has a feature that allows examiners to instruct youths with regard to that element and then examine their capacity to comprehend and recall the information. This is not done for everything the youth does not understand, but merely for a few elements in order to test the youth's potential to learn what he or she does not seem to grasp.

Sometimes youths initially lack factual understanding of some elements of the adjudicative process, yet are fully capable of understanding and appreciating them if they are provided a bit of instruction. In such cases, sometimes a finding of incompetence can be avoided if it is apparent that the youth has the capacity to learn, given that counsel simply describes to the youth those matters with which the youth is not familiar. This feature of the JACI provides the examiner the opportunity to perform this sort of "capacity check."

Youths' responses to these "capacity checks" indicate only that they could retain and verbalize the necessary information immediately after it was described to them. It does not assure that they can retain the new information over a longer period of time for use during the trial process. An advantage of having a second interview with youths a few days later is that examiners can check to determine whether the youth was able to retain the information that was taught in the first interview.

Decision-Making Abilities

The JACI includes several problem-solving or decision-making vignettes that present youths with hypothetical circumstances (such as deciding how to plead, or deciding about a possible plea agreement), asking them to make a choice and explain their reasons for it. Here the focus is on their ability not only to have understood the information, but also to process it to arrive at a meaningful choice. What the youth actually chooses is of little consequence for competence to stand trial. But when youths make choices based on impulse, faulty beliefs, or completely on short-term outcomes (e.g., "I'd plead guilty so that I could go home tonight"), the fact that their reasoning appears to be based on immature notions of the circumstances may be relevant for the court to consider in weighing the issue of competence.

Structured "Tests" of
Competence to Stand Trial Abilities

The JACI is a convenient interview procedure that guides the examiner's inquiry with the youth. But it does not provide scores or other objective ways to compare youths' abilities to those of other youths or adults. To date no instruments of the latter type have been developed specifically for use with juveniles. In the absence of such instruments, some juvenile competence examiners employ competence to stand trial instruments that have been developed for adults.[34] Most of them employ questions that cover abilities similar to those in the JACI, but offer ways to score or rate the defendant's answers. Examiners must use them with caution, recognizing their limitations when applied to juveniles. Moreover, some of the instruments assess only a limited number of abilities within the *Dusky* domain, some ask questions that are not relevant to juvenile court (or fail to ask questions that are relevant), and (at the time of publication of this guide) none provides methods for comparing youths' scores to those of other youths of various ages. However, they do allow the examiner to compare a youth's score to those of adult defendants. This may be helpful when the legal standard for competence that is being applied in the youth's case requires an "adult level" of abilities.

---

[34] There are many competence to stand trial instruments that have been devised for use with adult defendants. For reviews, see Chapter 4 in: Thomas Grisso, *Evaluating Competencies: Forensic Assessments and Instruments* (2nd ed., 2003). Those that appear to be employed with some frequency with juveniles are: Norman Poythress et al., *The MacArthur Competence Assessment Tool-Criminal Adjudication: Professional Manual* (MacCAT-CA: 1999); Richard Rogers et al., *Evaluation of Competence to Stand Trial-Revised* (ECST-R: 2002); and Carolyn Everington and Ruth Luckasson, *Competence Assessment for Standing Trial for Defendants With Mental Retardation* (CAST-MR: 1992).

Part IV

USING CLINICIANS' OPINIONS

When examiners have completed their evaluation, they write a report that describes their evaluation and their opinions. The following discussions address several of the features of these reports, focusing especially on preparing judges and attorneys to evaluate and interpret them in deciding about youths' competence and remediation.

EXAMINERS' REPORTS
AND OPINIONS

The quality of examiners' written reports in juvenile competence cases is very important, because oral expert testimony by mental health examiners in juvenile court hearings is apparently very rare.[35] Reports of competence to stand trial evaluations should include the following types of information:

- the specific reason for the evaluation, as provided by the court or counsel requesting the evaluation
- the examiner's methods (listing all interview sessions, tests, records reviewed)
- the clinical and developmental information that was obtained, including the sources of that information
- a description of the youth's performance (adequacies and deficits) on the examination of specific abilities related to the *Dusky* standard
- the examiner's opinions regarding the youth's capacities (e.g., the examiner's interpretation of the information from the JACI as well as clinical and developmental information)

---

[35] Thomas Grisso and Judith Quinlan, supra note 17.

- the reasoning that led to the examiner's opinions
- if the youth has serious deficits in competency abilities, the potential for remediation of those deficits if the court finds the youth incompetent, where remediation is most appropriately done, and how long it might take

The Nature of the Examiner's Explanations

The requirement regarding "reasoning that led to the examiner's opinions" is too often overlooked by examiners. When examiners state their opinions (e.g., "Based on the clinical data, it is my opinion that this youth is poorly prepared to assist counsel . . ." or ". . . is unable to understand the nature of the proceedings"), they must explain how the data led to those opinions. *When those explanations are absent, courts and attorneys should require that they be provided.* To do less makes the examiner the fact finder, rather than the court.

There are several ways in which the examiner's explanation should clarify the issue for the court. First, what were the most important data or observations that led to the opinion that the youth has adequate abilities, or that suggested that the youth has serious deficits in competency abilities? Second, if there were significant deficits in the youth's abilities, what is the most likely cause of those deficits? If the cause appears to be a mental disorder, or developmental immaturity, how do these factors appear to be related to the deficits in abilities? After all, the mere fact that a youth has deficits in competency abilities, and has a mental disorder or seems immature, does not necessarily mean that the disorder or immaturity is responsible for the deficits. For example, what is the evidence that the youth is not feigning disability?

The Examiner's Opinion About Competence

Examiners do not always conclude their reports with an opinion concerning whether the youth "is competent" or "is not competent." This is sometimes perplexing to courts and attorneys, and it may be helpful to recognize some reasons why a bottom-line opinion of this sort sometimes is absent.

First, even after a thorough job of data collection, the facts in some cases simply are ambiguous or contradictory. In such cases, an examiner's effort to report that the youth is or is not competent would be misleading or a misrepresentation of the clinical evidence as the examiner sees it.

Second, some examiners believe that it is not proper for mental health professionals to provide an opinion on the "ultimate legal question" in any case. They believe that this requires that one form an opinion concerning whether the legal criteria for competence to stand trial have been met, that this is not a clinical question, and therefore that it is not within the proper boundaries for which they have been qualified as mental health experts.

Third, examiners for competency cases in juvenile courts currently are faced with uncertain standards for offering such opinions. As noted in Part I, in many juvenile courts it is as yet unclear whether the degree of ability required for competence to stand trial is the same as for adults in criminal court. Should courts be comparing youths to their peers in juvenile court, or to adults, when considering whether they are "capable enough" to participate in their juvenile court adjudication? Without legal guidance on this point, examiners may find it difficult to conclude that the youth "is competent" or "is not competent," even if they can clearly describe the youth's specific deficits in competency abilities and are willing to express an opinion on the legal conclusion.

When examiners do not offer an opinion as to the youth's "competence" or "incompetence," courts and attorneys are encouraged to explore with the examiner the reason for declining to form an expert opinion on this "ultimate legal question."

MENTAL DISORDERS AND DISABILITIES AND THEIR IMPLICATIONS FOR COMPETENCE

Youths' mental disorders and mental disabilities do not always translate directly into deficits in competency abilities. But sometimes they do, and a substantial variety of disorders may interfere with youths' abilities such as those that are assessed on the JACI. The following discussions provide some examples that may assist courts and attorneys in understanding the causes of competency deficits in juveniles as described by examiners.[36]

---

[36] Clinicians have at their disposable standard definitions of these mental disorders (e.g., American Psychiatric Association, *Diagnostic and Statistical Manual of Mental Disorders –* 4th Edition [*DSM-IV*: 1994]), as well as methods to obtain reliable diagnoses of these disorders among youths. Nevertheless, there is inherently greater error in the diagnosis of mental disorders among adolescents than among adults. For a description (written for the nonclinician) of the values and limits of diagnostic categories and methods with adolescents in juvenile justice custody, see Chapters 2 and 3 in: Thomas Grisso, *Double Jeopardy: Adolescent Offenders With Mental Disorders* (2004).

Mental Retardation

Diagnosis of mental retardation requires a valid measure of intelligence (with an intelligence test) indicating an IQ below 70, as well as evidence of significant impairment in functioning in everyday life. Youths with seriously impaired intellectual abilities often have poorer understanding of the purposes, procedures, and participants in trials than youths of the same age with better intellectual capacity. Some youths with mental retardation may be able to benefit from the "capacity checks" in the JACI, but often they will show little or no retention an hour or a week later. Youths with mental retardation often will manifest impaired reasoning ability as well. Thus they may manifest significant difficulties when processing the "Reasoning and Decision Making" items in the JACI.

Attention-Deficit/Hyperactivity Disorder

The tendency to be drawn off task by distracting stimuli, often seen in youths with ADHD, sometimes impairs a youth's ability to attend to questions, remain in the context of a discussion or a social event, and generally to "stay focused." Such symptoms can be responsible for irrelevant or tangential answers to JACI Understanding and Appreciation questions. Some youths with ADHD may respond impulsively, giving answers before a question has been completed, or providing answers to different but related items that are inconsistent.

Mood Disorders

Clinical levels of depression may retard the energy and thought processes of youths, resulting in apathetic, poorly motivated performance when answering questions such as those in the JACI. Depression may also color the youth's perceptions of the trial and defense consultation, so that choices seem to be based on pessimism rather than a broader consideration of the possibilities. It should be remembered that depression in youths very often manifests itself in anger. Depressed youths' sullen appearance may accompany a resistance to investing themselves in any consideration of the trial process, thus impairing their performance on the JACI.

Anxiety Disorders

Youths with anxiety disorders (such as Posttraumatic Stress Disorder) often manifest withdrawal, excessive cautiousness, and fearfulness. Sometimes their responses to JACI questions can be impaired by their passivity or reticence to engage the task. They may also manifest perceptions of participants in the trial process in fearful ways, more so than is seen in the ordinary dependency that is expected among younger youths in general.

Thought Disorders

Youths with schizophrenia or other disorders that include delusions and hallucinations are not often encountered in the juvenile justice system. This is partly because the symptoms of schizophrenia (sufficient to meet the criteria for that diagnosis) are only rarely seen in adolescence. In addition, youths with adolescent precursors of schizophrenia often are diverted to mental health services rather than adjudicated. But cases of youths with bizarre ideation do sometimes arise. Youths with early signs of schizophrenia (usually between ages 15 and 18) typically manifest bizarre if not fully delusional ideas, as well as disorganized processing of information. Thus their perceptions of their offenses, the consequences of adjudication, and the trial process and its participants may include odd, illogical, and inconsistent ideas. These may be subtle, not revealing themselves unless the examiner asks follow-up questions.

DEVELOPMENTAL IMMATURITY AND ITS IMPLICATIONS FOR COMPETENCE

As noted early in this guide, age is not necessarily a good way to assess a youth's cognitive or psychosocial maturity. Youths develop cognitive and psychosocial capacities at various rates, and one sometimes encounters relatively "mature" 14 year olds and relatively "immature" 17 year olds. Evidence for immaturity always rests on an analysis of the youth's actual functioning. For purposes of competency evaluations, the evidence for immature thought and perception is most relevant when it is seen in the context of the youth's answers to questions such as those in the JACI.

The following discussion provides examples of ways in which immature psychosocial functioning influences youths' competence to stand trial. This case is taken directly from the practice guide for clinicians, and it describes a youth's answers to specific questions in the JACI. Note that each example proceeds from an "understanding" question (comparable to "factual understanding") to an "appreciation" question (relevant for "rational understanding"). Seeing these together will provide a feel for the difference between the two, as well as for the importance of "appreciation" questions in assessing a youth's capacities to participate meaningfully in the trial.

The following case description is not a complete interview, and it does not contain examples of youths' "adequate" understanding or appreciation. The responses were selected specifically to illustrate a number of ways in which immature perspective may influence youths' notions of trials and decisions that defendants often must make. Note also that these examples by themselves do not signify "incompetence," nor would it be appropriate to conclude on the basis of these responses alone that this youth is competent or incompetent to stand trial. The question of legal competence would require consideration of other information as well – for example, the youth's adequate responses to other parts of the interview, whether the case is in juvenile or criminal court (presuming that different degrees of ability might be required in one versus the other), or other clinical and developmental information about the youth. Finally, readers should note that for some of the following examples, immaturity is only one possible explanation for the youth's response.

In the case[37] from which the following dialogue was taken, a 14-year-old male non-Hispanic white youth was examined in the presence of his mother and his defense attorney. The youth was in seventh grade, with special education beginning in second grade. His mother said that she and her husband had been diagnosed with Bipolar Disorder and that she had also been given a diagnosis of Attention-Deficit/Hyperactivity Disorder in childhood. The youth had been given both of these diagnoses at age 10. He was charged with assault (hitting a teacher), his first charged offense, although he had been reported to the juvenile court twice since age 12 for fighting that did not result in arraignments (the referrals were handled informally by intake probation officers).

Understanding: What is the name of the offense you are charged with?

They called it assault. (Examiner inquires.)
Said I hit a teacher.

Appreciation: Would people consider that a serious offense or not so serious?

---

[37] The youth's characteristics have been changed to protect confidentiality.

> *It happens all the time . . . people get into*
> *fights . . . it's not so serious.* (Examiner
> inquires.) *All my friends get into fights all the*
> *time.*

The youth knows the charges. However, when examined for
Appreciation of the significance of the charge, the youth applies an
inappropriate benchmark for judging its seriousness from a social
perspective, because the charge involved an alleged assault against an
adult in authority, not a scuffle with a peer. Several hypotheses are possible.
It is possible that this is a youth with antisocial tendencies who perceives
assault as a common and ordinary event in life. Alternatively, the youth
might be operating at a level of cognitive development that is somewhat
concrete and simplistic. He may not yet discriminate that the seriousness
of an act (hitting) might be perceived differently depending on whether it
is unprovoked, occurs during a consensual fight, or is directed toward
persons in authority.

Understanding: Before a juvenile court trial, defendants are
asked whether they plead "guilty" or "not
guilty." What does "pleading guilty" mean?

Guilty means admit to the crime. Not guilty
means you don't admit it.

Appreciation: What will happen at court if you plead guilty
("admit to the offense")? Or if you don't plead
guilty ("do not admit to the offense")?

If you plead guilty, you'll get sentenced. If you
plead not guilty, you say you are innocent.
(What will happen then?) *I don't know. I guess*
you will get let go.

Appreciation: If you actually did the thing the police say you
did, can you plead not guilty?

I would plead not guilty, because I didn't hurt
the teacher. (What if you did hurt her?) *Well, I*
guess I'd have to plead guilty. (Examiner
inquires.) *Because if you did it, then you have*
to tell the truth. (Examiner inquires.) *You can't*
lie in court – you have to tell the truth or you
get in trouble.

> [Later in the JACI during the item that examines the youth's perceptions of the judge's role, the youth understands that the judge "makes the final decision." But. . . .]
>
> If the judge said you must tell the court whether or not you did what the police said, what would you do?
>
> *I guess tell them.* (Examiner inquires.) *Cause he's the judge – you got to.*

This youth understands that a guilty plea means that one admits to the crime and that a not-guilty plea means that one does not. However, the answers to the two Appreciation questions suggest that the youth perceives a plea as the defendant's description of what actually happened. (That is, one must plead "the truth.") It is not uncommon for youths at an early stage of adolescent development (and for children younger than adolescence) to presume that it is wrong not to speak the truth when adults confront them about their behavior. Many youths might lie, but most of them recognize that it is wrong and would not willingly tell another authority (here, the examiner) that lying is acceptable.

Pleading not guilty when one has actually done what is charged is interpreted concretely by many youths as "a lie," not as a choice that requires the state to prove the allegations. Two psychosocial developmental factors may be at play here – the development of abstract abilities, and deference to authority (lack of perceived autonomy).

> **Understanding**: What things could happen to you if a juvenile court judge found you guilty?
>
> *Could go to juvenile hall?* (Examiner inquires.) *Jail for kids.*
>
> **Appreciation:** What is the worst thing that the court could do. . . ?
>
> *Give me community service in the winter, cause it's cold out. I'd have to chop ice.* (Examiner inquires.) *Someone told me you have to chop ice off the sidewalks.*

Appreciation: What is the worst punishment your parent(s) has ever given you?

Making me clean my room . . . wash up everything, put everything away, all that stuff. I had to do it last week and now I have to do it again this afternoon.

Which would you rather do – clean up your room or go to juvenile hall?

Go to juvenile hall. (Examiner inquires.) *I hate to clean my room . . . I have to do it all the time.*

Would you rather clean up your room or do community service in the winter?

Community service.

He seems to have a simple Understanding of some of the possible consequences of adjudication. However, one wonders about his ability to Appreciate their significance, and therefore to make meaningful choices about consequences that might arise from decisions he makes (e.g., about pleas). A number of factors associated with immaturity might be at play here. One is the immediacy of having to clean his room ("this afternoon") in contrast to the hypothetical (and relatively remote) nature of the other punishments. The latter would undoubtedly be more onerous if they were to occur. But the youth's immature time perspective may focus on what is real and immediate rather than what is only possible and distant. Incomplete development of the ability to think about abstractions – things that do not currently exist in one's life and have not been experienced before – may also impair the youth's ability to engage in effective "what-if" imagining of the hypothetical punishments.

Understanding: What does a defense lawyer do?

Make sure you don't get in trouble. (Examiner inquires.) *She proves that you're innocent.* (Examiner inquires.) *She's on your side.*

(Defense attorney spontaneously asked) How do I do that?

I don't know.

Appreciation: Are there ways your lawyer might hurt your case?

She might tell the truth. (Examiner inquires.) *I don't know . . . I'm getting confused.*

Imagine that your defense lawyer said to you, "I want you to tell me what happened the night you were arrested." Why would the lawyer want to know that?"

So she knows what to tell the judge. (Examiner inquires.) *She would have to tell him what I did.*

[From a later portion of the section on "Assisting the Defense Attorney"]

Understanding: What are some things you can think of that you might do in order to help your lawyer to defend you?

Tell her what happened, who was there, things like that.

Appreciation: Imagine a defendant just didn't want to talk to the lawyer. Why could that be a problem?

Cause they are guilty . . . they did it. (Examiner inquires.) *If they don't talk to their lawyer, they must be guilty.*

Note that if one were simply investigating the youth's "factual understanding," the youth's responses would provide little concern. He said that the attorney helps the defendant, she tries to "make sure you don't get in trouble," proves you are innocent, and she needs to have information from the defendant in order to do her job. It is only in the Appreciation inquiries that the youth's clear misperception of the defense attorney's role comes clear. The misperception includes several interesting notions. One is that defense counsel protects the defendant, but only if the defendant has not committed the crime that is charged. The other is that the defense attorney is, in effect, responsible for aiding the state in securing a conviction if the defendant actually committed the charged crime.

It is neither uncommon nor surprising that some youths have the notion that the defense attorney is someone who helps you and yet might do things that will lead to your punishment. This is precisely what many youths experience when their parents protect them from everyday harms, yet approve of a school's punishment of them when they do something for which they need to accept responsibility and the consequences. The dependent status of youths makes it difficult for many of them to manage the concept that an adult (the defense attorney) would confront other adults (the state or the court) in order to assist a youth in potentially avoiding the consequences of the youth's wrongful behavior.

> [From a section of the JACI called "Deciding about a Plea Bargain," after the plea options and consequences have been described. A plea of guilty will get probation and, if re-arrested, a term in a juvenile correctional facility.]
>
> Now, let's say that your lawyer tells you she can't promise that it will actually happen, but there is a pretty good chance you could be found not guilty and not have any punishment. . . .
>
> (Youth interrupts.) *I'd plead not guilty.*
>
> . . . although it might take a little while before the judge can schedule a trial, and you'll be in detention during that time.
>
> *No way . . . I'd plead guilty.*
>
> Why would you take the plea?
>
> *I don't want to spend no time locked up.*
>
> If you plead guilty and go on probation, and if you get in trouble during that time, you'll have to go to juvenile lock-up.
>
> *That won't happen . . . I'd take my chances.*

The sequence of responses here suggests that the youth favors avoiding detention now and risking longer range sentencing to secure corrections, even though briefer, immediate detention is likely to lead to acquittal on the charges. This choice might be a consequence of several developmental factors, such as shortened time perspective, an immature perception of risk ("It won't happen to me"), and a tendency to focus one-sidedly on immediate gains despite the possibility of more serious long-range losses.

Note, however, that we cannot be sure that his choice is a consequence of immaturity. After all, many adults (presumably mature) might make the same choice. The hypothesis regarding developmental immaturity as a "cause" will require additional evidence from other sources that the youth consistently manifests these features of psychosocial immaturity in other circumstances.

This case, then, provides an example of how examiners might think and reason about the relation between immature psychosocial characteristics of youths and their capacities to participate in their defense. How these aspects of developmental immaturity will be weighed by the court depends, of course, on evolving law regarding the relevance of developmental immaturity as a possible cause for incompetence to stand trial. From a practical perspective, however, youths' deficits related to immaturity often will have the same consequence – inability to meaningfully assist counsel or understand the proceedings – as deficits due to mental illness or mental retardation.

RESPONSES TO FINDINGS
OF INCOMPETENCE

Recall from Part I that many jurisdictions specify a limit to the time that is allowed to remediate a defendant's incompetence to stand trial. In states in which this is the case, if the youth's incompetence is potentially remediable within the time provided by law, the court orders an appropriate referral for remediation services. If the court finds that the youth's incompetence is not likely to be remediated within the statutory time period, the charges typically must be dismissed and the delinquency (or criminal) proceeding terminated. As noted in Part I, law has not yet provided adequate guidance for many of the dispositional questions in juvenile competence cases. Moreover, there are significant variations in procedures and options across jurisdictions. Therefore, the following discussion offers only general guidance for remediation of incompetence in juvenile cases.

Incompetence Due to
Mental Disorder

When youths' incompetence to stand trial arises because of deficits caused by their mental disorders, the disposition will often involve treatment of their disorders in order to reduce symptoms that are interfering with their abilities associated with the competence standard. In those cases, examiners' reports will already have described the nature and severity of the youth's disorders. In addition, the remediation question before the court should be informed by the following opinions of the examiner:

- what is likely to be required in order to treat the mental disorder
- the likelihood that the youth's condition can be remediated sufficiently to increase competency abilities
- how long that is expected to require
- where such treatment can take place (which should be in the least restrictive setting, taking into account public safety and the youth's interests)

In the case of adolescents in criminal court, the designation of a place for inpatient treatment will often raise dilemmas. Most incompetent adults with mental disorders may be remanded to a forensic psychiatric inpatient facility designed for treatment to restore competence in the context of appropriate security. But many states' laws will not (or should not) allow a youth to be sent to an adult forensic psychiatric facility, partly because neither the treating professionals nor the setting are likely to be appropriate to treat psychiatric disorders of children and adolescents.[38]

How this dilemma is resolved will depend largely on jurisdictional circumstances. One approach is to require that youths in such cases are sent to general (nonforensic) child psychiatric inpatient facilities for treatment. In some jurisdictions, such facilities will be accustomed to receiving youths from juvenile courts where they have been found incompetent. In other communities, however, they may be unfamiliar with legal requirements regarding continued reassessment of the youth's progress and notification of the court when the youth achieves competence. Thus these arrangements may require close monitoring by the court and the attorneys on a case-by-case basis.

---

[38] Some adult forensic hospitals may have separate juvenile forensic psychiatric units, in which case commitment to that hospital may be appropriate, as long as the clinical staff serving the juvenile forensic unit are specialized in the treatment of child and adolescent mental disorders.

Incompetence Due to Developmental
Immaturity or Mental Retardation

When youths' incompetence to stand trial arises because of deficits caused by developmental immaturity or mental retardation, the course for remediation is far less clear than for mental disorder. In these cases, examiners' competency reports will already have described the nature of the immaturity, or nature and severity of mental retardation. In addition, to address the remediation question, they should describe:

- whether the specific deficiencies in competence abilities are likely to be remediable, in light of the cause;
- if so, how long it is likely to take to bring about remediation; and
- where such treatment can take place.

Concerning the questions above, there are some cases in which the deficiencies might be remediable within the statutory limit for remediation of competence, and other cases in which they might not be remediable. When the primary deficit is the youth's poor factual understanding, several studies have shown that programs designed specifically for educating youths regarding the relevant aspects of trials can remediate those deficits.[39] However, most jurisdictions have no such programs.

In addition, some youths' deficits in competence abilities are not a question of poor factual understanding, but rather immature capacities for appreciation or decision making – for example, immature processing of information or decision making that is influenced by psychosocial or cognitive immaturity (e.g., impulsiveness, foreshortened time perspective, as yet undeveloped capacity for abstract thinking). There is little evidence that such things can be "taught" before a youth has sufficiently matured in the ordinary progress of adolescent development.

These latter cases produce a significant dilemma. In criminal court cases, most states for several decades have had laws requiring that incompetent defendants' charges must be dismissed if their incompetence is not remediable within the legal time limits.[40] Often these time limits – in some states, a year – are not enough time for most youths to "mature" sufficiently to change their developmental status. Criminal courts could

---

[39] For example, see Annette McGaha et al., *Juveniles Adjudicated Incompetent to Proceed: A Descriptive Study of Florida's Competence Restoration Program*, 29 Journal of the American Academy of Psychiatry and Law 427 (2001).

[40] States' laws in this area were significantly influenced by *Jackson v. Indiana*, 406 U.S. 715 (1972), which required limits on the length of criminal confinement for treatment of incompetence to stand trial.

"waive" such youths to juvenile court for trial, providing that the threshold for competence to stand trial in juvenile court is lower than the threshold in criminal court (see discussion on pages 5-7 in Part I, "What Is the Legal Standard?"). If the threshold in juvenile court is the same as in criminal court, however, then criminal courts would seem to have no other option but to dismiss the charges.

If youths are found incompetent in juvenile court, the dilemma is similar, but some states have found a resolution by calling for dismissal of charges and referral to the child welfare jurisdiction of the juvenile court.[41] Most youths found incompetent due to immaturity will be young (i.e., under 15). And most youths found incompetent due to mental retardation may qualify for a variety of special community services. Therefore, while charges may be dismissed, in most cases involving immature youths, juvenile courts may exercise their civil powers to construct a plan that involves an appropriate arrangement of custodial and treatment services that serve the youth and protect the community. And in cases involving incompetence due to mental retardation, similar arrangements (also assuring public protection and youth services) often can involve the array of services available in the community for youths with developmental disabilities.

---

[41] For specific jurisdictions, see Richard Redding and Linda Frost, supra note 9.

IN CLOSING

This guide for legal professionals has been written to assist them in understanding and using mental health professionals' evaluations of youths' competence to stand trial. Reflecting on the legal and clinical discussions in the guide, lawyers and judges will note that this evaluation task presents clinicians with a number of difficulties. Competence to stand trial in juvenile court has been recognized as a right in delinquency cases only very recently. As a consequence, legal standards for competence in juvenile court are often ambiguous, making it difficult for clinicians to use the law as guidance when deciding how they should perform their evaluations. Moreover, although forensic clinicians have a long history of performing competence to stand trial evaluations in criminal court with adult defendants, only some of that experience is applicable for evaluations of children and adolescents. Evaluating juveniles' competence to stand trial is a relatively new task for forensic mental health professionals.

The newness of the task is what gave rise to the need to publish *Evaluating Juveniles' Adjudicative Competence: A Guide for Clinical Practice*, a companion to the present guide for legal professionals. The clinicians' guide discusses the same principles and methods, in greater detail, that are described in the present guide. However, the clinicians' version is the first work to offer forensic mental health professionals a comprehensive description of the legal and clinical issues they face in this area of forensic evaluation. It also offers the first extensive discussion of specialized strategies and methods for performing evaluations of juveniles' competence to stand trial.

Therefore, the clinicians' and legal professionals' guides describe what may be considered an emerging or potential standard for competence evaluations in juvenile court. They do not describe average or standard practice at the time these guides were published, but rather a proposal for practice to which clinicians may aspire. Clinicians who accept that challenge can be greatly assisted by attorneys and judges who recognize the relevance of clinicians' careful, developmentally sensitive approach to evaluating youths' competence to stand trial. The publication of these parallel guides for mental health and legal professionals will have been fruitful if they contribute to the professions' mutual understanding of the importance of well-constructed evaluations in the interest of due process for youths in delinquency proceedings.